FORGIVENESS

FORGIVENESS

PERSPECTIVES ON MAKING PEACE WITH YOUR PAST

Compiled and introduced by
Amy Lyles Wilson

FRESH AIR BOOKS™
Nashville

Contents

INTRODUCTION
Amy Lyles Wilson

The test of forgiving lies with healing the lingering pain of the
past, not with forgetting that the past ever happened.

—Lewis B. Smedes

"Forgive and forget," my mother told me when I came home from
junior high school in tears on an especially hot day in August.
After weeks of practicing my baton twirls and my marching steps, I
had not been chosen for the band's drill team. I was a half beat behind
from the get-go out there on the dry football field, and I knew I was
toast. To this day I'm not even sure why I wanted to be a flag girl,
except that I was not pretty enough for the beauty pageant or popular
enough for the cheerleading squad. And when a girl I considered less
graceful was chosen and I was not, I was devastated.

After I stopped emitting the loud sobs that only wronged
teenagers can produce, Mother took me on a walk through the

neighborhood and encouraged me to consider that maybe, just maybe, this was not the end of the world. Somehow, by the time we'd gone around the block a few times, I had regained my will to live—or at least enough gumption to face another day in the school cafeteria. I wasn't sure how I would ever forgive the band director or forget my humiliation, but eventually the hurt lessened, no doubt overshadowed by not being invited to the prom and losing the student council election.

Now having lived over four decades, I have endured much tougher experiences that required forgiveness. Like many of you, I've been dealt a few cards I do not think I deserved. In response, I used to think forgiving and forgetting meant I had to act like I had never been wronged. The writers in this collection tell me otherwise. Forgiving, they say, does not require pretending you were never hurt. It does mean, however, that you'll need to make peace with your past in order to embrace the future.

Forgiveness: Perspectives on Making Peace with Your Past guides us to an understanding that acknowledges human nature and celebrates God's grace. From defining forgiveness to learning to forgive ourselves, these essays provide insight and encouragement for the journey toward healing.

A FRESH ACT
Douglas V. Steere

Forgiveness is a condition in which the sin of the past is not altered or its inevitable consequences changed. Rather, in forgiveness a fresh act is added to those of the past, which restores the broken relationship and opens the way for the one who forgives and the one who is forgiven to meet and communicate deeply with each other in the present and future. Thus, forgiveness heals the past, though the scars remain and the consequences go on. These keep the sinner humble. But now the past can no longer throttle. It is taken into the fresh act of outgoing renewal and there it is healed.

A BITTER ROOT
Mary Lou Redding

It is easy to avoid dealing with painful issues in our lives by saying that the time is not right. That allows us to push away (banish) the pain and the persons who have hurt us and to continue to deny that we have been hurt and are still hurting. When is the right time? The right time is whenever we become aware that pain from old wounds is leaking into today, interfering with life. That awareness is God calling to us, asking us if we want to be free and to move forward with our lives. If we do, God offers us a way to do so. It's a process called forgiveness.

∾

One of the most difficult things for me to understand about human nature is how we cling to our pain. Sometimes it is almost as if it defines who we are. If we let go of it, who will we be?

What will draw the outlines of our life? I think about my mother and her painful life. She grew up desperately poor in the hardscrabble culture of Kentucky coal-mining towns, and life was difficult. Her mother left her and her brother when they were preschoolers and died when Mother was nine years old. While her dad worked in the coal mines, she and her brother lived with relatives who mostly didn't want them.

Mother was never able to let go of the view that the world is a harsh and unfriendly place and that life is mostly struggle. I always wished that she could see the world as a more welcoming place. Maybe she could have been more welcoming toward others if she had. But she could not let go of the great pain she had endured, and she was critical and pessimistic about human nature and about life. Her pain both defined and limited who she was.

I thought of her often as I struggled to come to terms with the end of my marriage. If I did not let go of the hurts of my marriage and subsequent divorce, I would also be shaped and limited by them. The pain had been great, but the hurts my husband, Spencer, and I had inflicted on each other had not sprung from malice. As his deep needs went unmet and his pain increased, he lashed out at me because I was the one who was there. He did not realize what he was doing. And even when he lashed out in malice, he did not realize how deeply his actions hurt me. I had to forgive him. If I did not, the hurt I carried would sour within me and turn into bitterness.

We do not have to wait for others to change or to ask for forgiveness. Jesus' example on the cross shows us this. When he prayed, "Father, forgive them; for they know not what they do" (Luke 23:34, KJV), he gave us a model that can transform our way of dealing with those who hurt us. We don't have to wait for them to repent and ask for our forgiveness. That may never happen. But we can forgive them and leave behind what they have done to us. I wanted to forgive, to leave the pain behind for good. I wasn't sure how I would know when I had done this.

As I talked with my counselor and prayed, I came to believe that Spencer was probably in as much pain as I was, maybe even more, and I began to pray for him. During our conversation about my filing for divorce, I had told Spencer I was sorry for hurting him, but I said that with little understanding of his pain. I had not really believed that

I had done much to hurt him during our marriage. Now I found myself wondering how he felt at losing his home. One of the two things we had going for us, according to our premarital counselor, was that we both deeply wanted marriage and a Christian home. Spencer adored our daughter, Emily, and I began thinking about the pain he must have felt at being separated from her. I found myself praying for him frequently. Many of the prayers were the same ones I had prayed before our divorce, but now I was praying those things for him, not out of the self-interest that had driven me to try to save our marriage. I was able to see and admit the good things about him and to acknowledge the good there had been in our marriage. When I was able to care about him and pray sincerely for God's best for him, then I knew I was truly free of the hurts that had built up over the years.

Being Less Than "Perfect"

There remained one more person to forgive: myself. The anger that was so close to the surface of my emotions had not come only because of what Spencer had done. I was also angry at me. I truly wanted to be perfect. Admitting the magnitude of my mistake in marrying made me feel stupid, and I really hate to feel stupid. In my way of looking at the world, other people are permitted to make mistakes, but I am not. I encourage others not to be too hard on themselves, but I have to do it right. Eventually, I came across something that helped me surrender that unattainable standard. Some sort of spiritual exercise led me through considering how I would help a close friend who was facing a struggle (I'm not even sure the struggle was a sin—just some sort of struggle). At the end of the exercise was a question something like, "Do you treat yourself this way when you are going through a struggle?" I saw that if God would want me to deal gently with others, I had to believe God wanted me to deal gently with myself too. I still remind myself of this strategy often. When I'm flogging myself mentally for something I've done, I stop and say to myself, "Would you treat your best friend this way?" I think of Frieda, my best friend, and realize I would try to be gentle and loving with her. Then I am able to be more loving toward myself.

I believe that God is continually guiding each of us toward forgiveness. God wants to mend our hearts that have been wounded in hurtful relationships and set us free to love without strings attached.

I know that God has acted that way in my life, and I have come to believe that it is a general spiritual principle. One of the people who convinced me of that was Spencer. One cold January afternoon a few years ago as I worked in my office, the phone rang.

"Mary Lou? This is Spencer."

"Well, hello!"

"Is this a convenient time for you to talk? Do you have a few minutes?"

"Sure. What do you need?"

"Well, I called because I want to ask your forgiveness."

He went on to ask forgiveness specifically for things he had done to hurt me during our marriage and while we were divorcing. Then he asked forgiveness for anything he had done in the years since to hurt me, ending with, "I'm sorry, and I ask you to forgive me if you can." For a few moments I was speechless (which is pretty rare for me). Finally I recovered my voice and told him that of course I forgave him, that I had done so many years earlier.

We talked a bit more, and I said to him, "May I ask why you are doing this now? I mean, why today? What happened to bring you to do this?" He had been praying during a prayer vigil at his church, and it occurred to him that though he had asked God to forgive him, he had never asked me to—and he felt he needed to do that. It had taken years—many years—after our divorce for us to come to this place, but I believe it was God's grace that brought us both here. In a later conversation Spencer told me that the experience was momentous for him. It came at a time in his life when spiritual change was taking place, and for him to call me was a big thing. He said, "It was the Lord who was working in me to bring me to that place."

Living into Forgiveness

The tension and animosity, the inner uneasiness, are gone. When we are together for important events in our daughter's life, we can share meals and laugh about our younger years. I inquire about his life, his family, his wife and stepchildren. We care about each other and can show care toward each other. I pray for him and his family, and I know he prays for me. We have talked about that.

This doesn't mean that I have never gotten annoyed at Spencer since then. He still does things in his relationship with Emily that I disagree with. But when I get angry with him, it is about things that are happening now, not things that I've saved up from long ago, and the anger doesn't last long or overwhelm me. In this relationship at least, the hurts of the past no longer contaminate the present.

My path and his in coming to this place have been very different, but I believe that God wants to guide each of us along a road that leads toward forgiveness. We know that not everyone chooses to face the pain he or she has suffered and inflicted. And sometimes the way is long and winding, especially when the hurts have been deep. But there is a wide, good place at its end. This is a gift of grace.

WHAT FORGIVENESS IS AND IS NOT
Kenneth Gibble

I t is important to understand what forgiveness is, but it's equally important to understand what forgiveness is not. Forgiveness is not forgetting. The memory of deep hurts will most likely last a lifetime.

Forgiveness is not dismissing the hurt, shrugging it off. "Aw, that's okay," you might say to someone who has hurt you, even though it is not okay at all. Forgiveness involves taking the offense seriously, not passing it off as insignificant.

Forgiveness is not condoning. You don't have to excuse the bad or hurtful thing done to you. And, if possible, you should not remain in a situation where continued danger exists (for example, when someone is physically abusive to spouse or children).

Forgiveness is not reconciliation. It takes two people for reconciliation to occur, and sometimes forgiveness does lead to reconciliation; but an injured party can forgive an offender even when reconciliation is not possible.

Forgiveness is none of those things. But it is something we are commanded to do. Forgiveness is always a decision. It's a decision not to seek revenge or nurse a grudge.

Sometimes it helps to tell yourself why you are deciding to forgive. For example, you might say, "I will forgive so that I can have inner healing and get on with my life." It is surely true that the first person who benefits from forgiveness is the person who does the forgiving.

One of the best ways of making forgiveness a reality is to pray for the welfare of the person who has caused you to suffer. That isn't easy, but it is one of the gifts God gives us in the healing that forgiveness makes possible. Forgiveness is a gift, God's gift, first of all, to each of us. And then a gift we give to others, a gift that, in the giving, brings to the giver unexpected and undeniable blessing.

Learning to forgive is not something that happens quickly or easily. Learning to forgive is a lifetime process. But it helps to remember that we are being forgiven every day of our lives. Forgiveness, as Barbara Brown Taylor has said, "is God's cure for the deformity our resentments cause us. It is how we discover our true shape, and every time we do it we get to be a little more alive."[1]

Forgiveness is hard, but it is not impossible. People who have learned to forgive are usually people who realize how forgiven they are. They can love because they have been loved.

THE FIRST LOVE
Henri J. M. Nouwen

The voice calling us the Beloved is the voice of the first love. By first love I mean the love that existed before any human love touched us. I have had to live many years to be able to speak about this first love because all my attention has been directed to the love that came from my parents, brothers, sister, friends, colleagues, and members of my community. When I am honest with myself, I can see that most of what I normally think, worry, and even agonize about has to do with human relationships. What makes me happy or sad is closely linked to what I think or feel about other people. But "other people" are precisely that: "other people," people who, like me, are very limited and can love only in a conditional way. The great tragedy of human love is that it always wounds. Why is this so? Simply because human love is imperfect, always tainted by needs and unfulfilled desires.

Isn't it true that the persons we love most and who love us most are also the persons who hurt us most? Think about parents, friends, spouses. Those who are closest to us are also those who cause us the deepest pain. Neither the strangers far away, even when we are aware of their struggles, nor the enemies close by, even when they hate or reject us, are the main source of our anguish. Strangers and enemies are outsiders. We do not give them access to our innermost being. No, our real anguish comes from those who love us but who cannot love us in the way our heart desires. It is our father, our mother, our brother, our sister, our spouse, our closest friend, our co-worker, our neighbor who can hurt us most and be most hurt by us. It is with good reason that counselors and therapists always deal with these primary relationships. That is where we are most loved and most wounded. That is where our greatest joy and our greatest pain touch each other.

Why do those who love us wound us so much? It is because they cannot fulfill our deep and often unconscious desire for complete communion. The first love, the love of the One who calls us the Beloved and offers us that complete communion, does not wound us.

God's love is unconditional, not limited by needs and unfulfilled desires. It is a love that freely gives without strings attached. By claiming that first love as real, and not just as wishful thinking, we can begin to live joyfully in a world where love is, and can only be, offered to us in a limited and conditional way, even by those who love us most.

Here we can catch a glimpse of the great mystery of forgiveness. Forgiveness is made possible by the knowledge that human beings cannot offer us what only God can give. Once we have heard the voice calling us the Beloved, accepted the gift of full communion, and claimed the first unconditional love, we can see easily—with the eyes of a repentant heart—how we have demanded of people a love that only God can give. It is the knowledge of that first love that allows us to forgive those who have only a "second" love to offer.

I am struck by how I cling to my own wounded self. Why do I think so much about the people who have offended or hurt me? Why do I allow them to have so much power over my feelings and emotions? Why can't I simply be grateful for the good they did and forget about their failures and mistakes? It seems that in order to find my place in life I need to be angry, resentful, or hurt. It even seems that these people gave me my identity by the very ways in which they wounded me. Part of me is "the wounded one." It is hard to know who I am when I can no longer point my finger at someone who is the cause of my pain!

But what if we realize that we are the Beloved long before anyone can wound us? What if we are the Beloved long before any person accepted or rejected us? What if our true name is not the name given to us by those whose love was so limited that they could not avoid hurting us? What if our true home is not the house we live in, but the sacred place in the unconditional love of the One whose being is pure love? Would there be any reason to cling to our negative feelings? Wouldn't they disappear like snow in the sun? Wouldn't forgiveness be the most spontaneous and even the easiest response?

This perspective does not underestimate the importance of exploring how and why we got wounded. It is important to understand our suffering. It is often necessary to search for the origins of our mental and emotional struggles and to discover how other people's actions and our response to their actions have shaped the way we think, feel, and act. Most of all, it is freeing to become aware that we do not have to be victims of our past and can learn new ways of responding. But there is a step beyond the recognition and identification of the facts of life. There is even a step beyond choosing how to live our own life story. It is the greatest step a human being can take. It is the step of forgiveness. Forgiveness is the name of love practiced among people who love poorly. The hard truth is that all of us love poorly. We do not even know what we are doing when we hurt others. We need to forgive and be forgiven every day, every hour—unceasingly. That is the great work of love among the fellowship of the weak that is the human family. The voice that calls us the Beloved is the voice of freedom because it sets us free to love without wanting anything in return. This has nothing to do with self-sacrifice, self-denial, or self-deprecation. But it has everything to do with the abundance of love that has been freely given to me and from which I freely want to give.

FORGIVING OURSELVES AND OTHERS
Wendy M. Wright

One of the most difficult challenges we seem to face in the spiritual journey is to love ourselves as we have been loved. There are many interpretations, both present and past, of the particularities of that challenge. I choose to focus on it from one vantage point. I call it the art of "loving our abjections." It is an art I have been exploring for a long time and one I suspect will be in need of constant practice until I die. The phrase comes from a seventeenth-century Salesian spiritual tradition whose chief architects are saints Francis de Sales and Jane de Chantal.

Our "abjections" are those limiting and limited aspects of all of our lives. They are the shadowy side, the weaknesses, the brokenness that is simply a part of who we are. We can kick at it, hide it, deny it; it will not go away. In fact, the more vehemently we ignore or despise it, the more energy we have to expend to convince others and ourselves that it does not exist. Instead, we need to learn to accept our very real limitations, to allow them into our purview. But the spiritual tradition of these saints went beyond this psychologically commonsense approach. It invited me to love my abjections.

I gradually came to see that I was being invited to love myself as God loved me, cognizant of the wholeness of who I am—both gifted and wounded, blessed and broken. I was being invited to forgive myself little by little for all I found unacceptable and wearisome in myself. After a time, I came to see that I was forgiving myself for simply being human. My past uncompromising self-censure suddenly seemed silly. Gradually, I came to see the profound and simultaneous blessedness and brokenness of others as well. Bit by bit, I could allow them both the fullness of their promise and the reality of their own serious limitations. Gradually, the deep ambiguity of human life was turned from a burdensome mystery into a freeing one. Freed from my energetic desires to constantly "get it" and "keep it together," I could genuinely allow God to work in and through my abjections, not to make them better or neaten them up but to allow me to be more compassionate, to judge others less, to serve them better.

❧

If forgiving ourselves is one face of the mystery of reconciliation, forgiving others is another. But genuine forgiveness is not an easily cultivated art. Especially when we have been gravely wounded by another person, our basic human dignity affronted, it is no simple task to forgive. Nor should it be done lightly. For we need also to recognize and affirm the anger, the pain, the betrayal, or the sense of injustice that we feel when genuinely hurt. Validating the injury that has occurred or acquiescing to the idea that we have rightfully been victims and deserving of our pain is not forgiveness.

Real forgiveness means balancing rightful outrage at injury with the courage to extend forgiveness to the other and unleash the bonds that hold us both enchained. But it comes slowly and, if the injury is deep, we often find ourselves coming back to the injury as the layers of our lives are peeled back and exposed in time. I think of a woman I know whose life had been cleft in two a decade earlier when her husband had reconnected with a woman he had loved in an earlier era. After much anguish, he decided to leave and return to his first love. For years this woman struggled, with the helpful aid of friends and counselors, to put her life back together, finally arriving at the point where she could let go and forgive, wishing the reunited couple well. To her dismay one Saturday she found herself seated behind her ex-husband and his now wife at the wedding of mutual acquaintances. All the old feelings she assumed she had laid aside flooded back, poisoning the air, causing her to close in on herself and withdraw her presence from the celebration. An unopened layer of her pain was laid freshly bare, calling for new courage, new generosity, new reaffirmation of her own dignity and right to be loved.

❧

There is nothing easy about forgiveness. It asks us to be unmade and refashioned anew. Again and again and again, time after time after time. Yet ultimately, forgiveness is healing, both for the one who is injured and for the one who injures.

A priest friend of mine who has worked for years as a hospital chaplain tells of his experience at a nationally known clinic for the mentally and emotionally disturbed. While many people were helped in the environment of the psychiatric clinic, one group of patients seemed unable to make any progress in their healing. They had in common the fact that they all had been wounded deeply and found themselves unable to forgive their offenders. After years of therapy, it came down to that bare truth. A team of well-trained and qualified ministers who were engaged in spiritual healing were called in as a last resort. Every one of the patients was able to identify an inability to forgive as the root of his or her illness. Some could find in themselves a desire to be delivered from their inability, sensing it to be the key to their own release from suffering. Some could find available to them at least a desire to desire the gift of forgiveness. Working long and lovingly with these persons in pain, the team of healing ministers was able to bring healing into the lives of many of these formerly incurably troubled lives. Not all of them were healed, but many were. The gift of forgiveness was the key that unlocked their pain and set them free.

How astonishing: that in releasing another from being bound and identified with pain, we release ourselves as well. We discover the deep truth of the story of the prodigal son (Luke 15:11-32)—that miraculous parable of God's loving homecoming offered for all God's children, no matter how far they have strayed, no matter how long they have been gone, no matter how deeply they are mired. There is always forgiveness. There is always welcome.

The invitation is for us to offer this to one another as well. In so doing we enter into the mystery of our intimate interconnection with one another and with God.

RELEASING IN LOVE
Roberta Porter

I remember one
passed from this earth
but present
in pain
remaining.

    I cannot confront
    in anger
    or in love;
    I cannot tell
    of the sorrow
    caused.

        With prayer
        and time
        I begin to see

I can still choose
to do the work
of forgiveness.

I can release the pain
to God,
respond
to healing love
and recognize
God's care for me
and the freedom
that comes
as I learn
from the pain
and
live on.

ACKNOWLEDGE THE RAGE
Elizabeth J. Canham

While we are to forgive our enemies
and pray for those who hurt us,
we usually can arrive at that place of forgiveness
only when we acknowledge
the vindictive rage we bear toward them.
In expressing our desire for revenge,
we tell God who we are—hurting, broken people
not yet able to relinquish our pain—
and we give the rage to God.

HOW DO I PROTECT MYSELF?
Kathleen Fischer

Forgiving requires that we deal honestly with the dark undercurrents and with the cruelty of bad relationships. When we see only the good in those closest to us, we leave ourselves open to abuse and vengeance. We can forgive others and at the same time take the steps necessary to ensure our own safety.

The question *Will I be hurt again?* arises not only in situations of violence and abuse but in the daily push-and-pull of life. Many people undertake the process of forgiving only when they are assured that it will not make them vulnerable to the offending person. They want no part of a forgiveness that exposes them to ongoing hurt. We must therefore understand what the gospel asks of us. It does not require us to remain in situations of danger or to put up with ongoing hurt. Protecting ourselves from harm is our right and duty.

Jesus himself practiced the advice he gave his disciples: "See, I am sending you out like sheep into the midst of wolves; so be wise as serpents and innocent as doves" (Matt. 10:16). Fully aware of the sin and evil in the world, Jesus did not walk into the traps of others. After he cleansed the Temple of the money changers, he knew his life was in danger and delayed going to Jerusalem until he was ready.

For Jesus, forgiveness is no rerun of the old order. It creates the conditions necessary for a fresh start. Being his disciples does not mean exposing ourselves again and again to the same old hurts. It does mean caring enough about relationships to take steps to live them differently.

Mistaken ideas about the requirements of forgiveness prevent us from being "wise as serpents." Read the following list of false beliefs that many people hold. Which of them endanger your safety or prevent you from forgiving?

Myths about Forgiveness

1. Forgiveness requires me to stay in an abusive or violent relationship.
Absolutely not. In situations of violence and abuse, safety must be the primary concern. If you or someone you know is in such a relationship, get professional help. Domestic violence is a complex and

potentially dangerous situation; those with the experience and skill to respond appropriately should handle it. The best course of action for both the battered and the batterer is referral to a professional counselor, because each needs specialized help. Become acquainted with sources of help in your area, such as domestic violence hotlines, emergency shelters for the battered, and treatment programs for those who batter. These resources can provide safety and wisdom for the battered and accountability and sanctions for an assaultive spouse.

Too often women seeking help with domestic abuse receive admonitions to forgive, return to their husbands, and make their marriages work. We should not press persons in these situations to forgive. A spouse may already blame herself for the violence or abuse: "It was my fault; I could tell when he was going to go into a rage. I just said something that set him off." If a woman's religious tradition tells her that a good wife submits to her husband; that patience, obedience, and gentleness are womanly virtues; that suffering is to be endured; and that nothing justifies leaving a marriage, then she needs sound spiritual counseling. Emphasis on keeping a family together at all costs ignores the fact that over time, without intervention, abusive behavior tends to increase in frequency and severity.

Fear of being hurt again is well-founded when the offense is intentional and repeated and the offender shows no repentance. Forgiveness then becomes a way for the abused person to heal and get internally free; however, reconciliation is not possible. Victims of family abuse may find that they cannot have a relationship with the abuser again, although, after healing work, they may no longer hate the abuser. Forgiveness may even give some the courage to leave a destructive relationship. Some family members are so dangerous, and the harm they cause so severe, that the abused persons have to isolate themselves from the offender, at least for a time.

Recall that forgiving starts with an honest look at how we have been hurt. It asks us to recognize the source of our pain. For a relationship to continue, the one forgiven must learn from past mistakes and thoroughly renounce them. Since false promises of such repentance are part of the cycle of domestic abuse, persons in these relationships may need help to avoid succumbing to them.

2. Forgiving is the same as being nice. Women are especially apt to confuse forgiveness with being nice. Being nice is not a Christian virtue. It is simply a socially acceptable way of dealing with situations, one that women have been taught to observe since they were little girls. And it can put them at risk of physical and emotional harm.

Forgiveness does not preclude self-defense, protecting ourselves from harm, or saying no when a boundary has been threatened. It does not prevent us from learning to stay safe around dangerous family members. Nor does it mean giving up claims to justice and compensation.

An ancient tale illustrates this truth. Long ago there was a village with a saint living nearby. As he walked among the hills one day, the saint encountered a snake lying in the grass. Fangs bared, the snake lunged at the holy man as though it would bite him. But when the saint smiled, the snake was stopped by his kindness. The saint suggested that the rattler quit biting the children of the village. He pointed out that the snake would be better liked and cause less harm.

The snake agreed to follow the holy man's suggestion because he sensed his power. A week passed. When the saint went walking again, he found the snake lying on the ground, surrounded by blood. The snake berated the saint for the advice that had almost killed him: "Look what happened to me when I took your advice. I am a bloody mess. Look what happened to me when I tried to be nice and not bite, and now everyone is trying to hurt me."

The saint replied, "I never told you not to hiss."[1]

To hiss is to set limits and take steps to protect ourselves when necessary. It is to insist that family members get treatment for addiction and serious mental illness. It recognizes that, as much as we may want to deny it, abusers, rapists, murderers, and thieves all belong to somebody's family. When that family is our own, we will neither help the person nor ourselves if we settle for being nice. Forgiving should not turn us into doormats.

Unfortunately some who are close to us, even in our own families, act like enemies toward us. In these situations, forgiving calls for something much more exacting than being nice. We must struggle again and again with dilemmas: What does it mean to love such enemies? How do we keep our anger toward them from petrifying into hatred and a desire for their destruction?

3. Forgiveness means forgetting the offense. You may think you have forgotten the way your sister-in-law criticized your parenting skills. Then you see her at the next family gathering and try to avoid talking to her. Forgiveness is not a form of amnesia.

In fact, remembering is important to our safety. If we forget, the pattern may repeat itself. A woman describes how her recent birthday started out to be a happy day. Then her daughter ripped into her, laying out all her faults. Now she fears talking to her daughter again. "I don't think I can take another attack like that. Am I really that miserable a mother?" She will not likely forget the event, nor will pretending that she has forgotten help her. Another woman sums up her view of the problem: "Family burns you. You go back, and they burn you again." These women need strategies for preventing such hurts from recurring. What can they change about the situations or their own actions? If they simply forget, they will walk right into the same pain again.

Forgiveness brings about a change of seasons. We do not completely forget the interval of pain, but we do not live forever in its frigid climate. We let go of anger and bitterness but maintain awareness that what was done to us was wrong. After a hurt, attitudes of caution will persist until trust has been rebuilt. As events play out over time, we discover whether or not our trust is well-founded.

4. *My world will be the same as before the hurt.* When a parent, spouse, or other family member hurts us, the incident shatters our bedrock assumptions about life. Such wounding brings us up against the meaning of suffering and evil. It shakes our trust, our belief in justice, our opinion of ourselves, our faith in the goodness of people, and our conviction that God will protect us against harm. It destroys the idealized images of marriage and family we once cherished. While going through a divorce, a man laments: "How can I believe in anything anymore if I can't trust this woman I lived so close to for twenty years? I've lost all faith in myself. Why didn't I notice what was going on?"

At such times we can truly pray with the psalmist:

Save me, O God,
   for the waters have come up to my neck.
I sink in deep mire,
   where there is no foothold;

I have come into deep waters,

> and the flood sweeps over me. (Psalm 69:1-2)

This is one reason why "I forgive" is not a phrase tossed out in passing. It reaches into all areas of our lives. We learn that it is possible to feel both love and anger toward the same person, a difficult concept for children but necessary for adults. We develop a new understanding of family, one that may have to incorporate infidelity, incest, theft, and lies. We relinquish attempts to understand fully the why of suffering, the desire to get to the bottom of the pain another has caused us.

Ultimately the answer to the question *Will I be hurt again?* is yes. At bottom, forgiveness offers love to someone who has betrayed that love in small or large ways. This healing process cannot fail to have a profound impact on us. Inevitably, it leads to new beliefs about ourselves and relationships. We now know what it is to take a chance on loving others, but we can also make better choices about whether a particular gamble is one we should take. Forgiving reveals more fully our own limits and sinfulness and those of other family members. The English essayist C. S. Lewis remarks in his book *The Four Loves* that if we choose to love at all, we become vulnerable: "Love anything, and your heart will certainly be wrung and possibly be broken." The only way to prevent vulnerability, he says, is to refuse to love at all. But a heart locked up safely in this way will change nonetheless: "It will not be broken; it will become unbreakable, impenetrable, irredeemable."[2]

Eventually we integrate the recurrence of hurt into our worldview. We know it will happen again, but the experience no longer shatters our world. Forgiving takes us into what the gospel describes as a Christlike maturity. Jesus knew the evil in the world but did not let it deflect him from love and action. He experienced betrayal but continued to trust; his commitment to his mission took him to the Cross. The wounds he endured were still present after the Resurrection, visible in his hands and feet but transformed. Jesus promises that our own resurrections, including those experienced in family life, will bring this same kind of healing. His promise undergirds our prayer as we attempt to honor both a concern for safety and the call to forgiveness.

THE JOURNEY
Jean M. Blomquist

I confess. I cannot forgive him. He has caused great pain in my life and in the lives of loved ones. Over the years his hurtful actions and words have become more subtle perhaps, but they still continue. I've tried to forgive. I've prayed that I might forgive. I've prayed for healing in this relationship. For years I've prayed for healing.

Healing has come slowly, and with it a sliver of forgiveness. But neither my healing nor my forgiveness is yet complete. The journey to forgiveness, I've learned, is sometimes a long one. Often it shares the road with the journey toward healing. Both require stamina, commitment, persistence, and much grace, to overcome resistance, doubt, fear, and painful brokenness.

Authentic forgiveness—deep-hearted, full-spirited forgiveness—cannot be forced. Inauthentic forgiveness—words spoken out of obligation or coercion without the heart's concurrence—is a lie. This lie may deceive both the forgiver and the forgiven, but it does not deceive God. Neither does it incarnate the divine intent of forgiveness: to remove the barriers to a holy and right relationship, where the Spirit can move freely, gladly, and creatively.

As I continue my journey toward forgiveness in this difficult relationship, I am both challenged and sustained by scripture. I feel judged by Jesus' injunction to forgive "seventy times seven" (Matt. 18:22, RSV) and inadequate in the face of his command, "Whenever you stand praying, forgive, if you have anything against anyone; so that your Father in heaven may also forgive you your trespasses" (Mark 11:25). Clearly, I am not sin-free, so why can't I forgive one who has sinned against me?

But scripture, especially the Crucifixion story, also gives me hope in the face of my inadequacy: Jesus, humiliated and in deep pain, hangs on the cross. People mill around, just itching to mock and heckle. As Jesus' physical, emotional, and spiritual pain deepens, he says not "I forgive you," but *"Father,* forgive them . . . " (Luke 23:34).

Jesus' words sustain me as I stumble along the road toward forgiveness. Now I pray, "God, help me to forgive. What I am yet unable to forgive, I ask you to forgive. Help me grow into the fullness of forgiveness."

I realize now that forgiveness is not an act of will, something I can grit my teeth and force myself to do. Forgiveness is, instead, an act of grace, and the source of that grace is God. The grace of forgiveness flows out of the heart of God, not only toward the forgiven but also into the forgiver. In asking for the grace of forgiveness, the stream of forgiveness begins to flow.

Though my relationship remains difficult, I trust that God works even here. Somehow, beyond the narrow boundaries of my heart, beyond the meager measure of my compassion, beyond the depth of my pain, God graciously and gently journeys with me toward forgiveness.

OUR RESISTANCE TO FORGIVENESS
Marjorie J. Thompson

Forgiveness constitutes a decision to call forth and rebuild that love which is the only authentic ground of any human relationship. Such love forms the sole secure ground of our relationship with God as well. Indeed, it is only because God continually calls forth and rebuilds this love with us that we are capable of doing so with one another. Thus, to forgive is to participate in the mystery of God's love. Perhaps this is why the old adage rings true: "To err is human; to forgive, divine." Genuine forgiveness draws us right into the heart of divine life.

Our Resistance to Forgiveness

But this brings us to our difficulty with forgiveness. We may be quite clear about what is called for but find ourselves unable or unwilling to do it. How do we release a person who has deeply wounded us from the sentence of our condemnation—a judgment that rises spontaneously, unbidden, from feelings of hurt, anger, fear, or resentment?

The experience of being unfairly or inhumanely treated usually leaves us with a desire for revenge. We may be inclined to return the wrong in kind, inverting the Golden Rule: "Do unto others as they have done unto you." We may prefer more sophisticated varieties of punishment that are expressed in oblique ways: withdrawing from the relationship, engaging in "passive aggression," or venting our anger in manipulation and deceit.

If lashing back is not our way of responding to hurt, it is probable that we at least expect restitution. The offender ought to do or say something to mend the hurt, to repay us for the loss of dignity and trust we have experienced. What, then, do we do if the culprit refuses even to acknowledge that a problem exists? How can we forgive if there is no contrition?

Of course it makes forgiving much easier if the offender is willing to admit guilt and ask for pardon. But can we make conscious admission and remorse a condition for the kind of forgiveness that reflects God's love? Jesus' words of forgiveness from the Cross were offered up freely for all who would receive them. Indeed, the reason he gives in that brief prayer for asking God's mercy is precisely that we "know not what we do."

If we don't comprehend the full impact, the true seriousness of our behaviors, how shall we know enough to ask forgiveness? More often than not, those who have hurt us do not comprehend the destructive magnitude of their behavior. We are called to offer unconditional forgiveness, as God in Christ offers it to us. Jesus tells Peter in Matthew 18:22 to forgive "seventy times seven," a hyperbole by which he indicates that those who wish to be his disciples should place no limits on their mercy. Nowhere does Christ exempt us from this call merely because the offending party has not confessed to sin.

This raises an important distinction between forgiveness and reconciliation, two intimately related but distinct spheres. Forgiveness, it seems, can be offered unilaterally, and therefore without conditions. I can forgive a friend who doesn't know she has hurt me; I can forgive a parent or grandparent who is no longer present on this earth; I can forgive persons or groups of persons without their consciously knowing it or having any way to respond.

My one-way forgiveness is a matter of releasing others from judgment in my own heart. Such unilateral forgiveness does more than release me from the corrosive burden of anger and bitterness that eats away my peace of soul, although this is certainly one of the great gifts inherent in forgiveness. It also removes any hidden or overt effects of resentment in my way of relating to the other, either person-to-person or with third parties. Moreover, I believe that hidden forgiveness affects the spirit of the person who has been released in ways that go beyond our comprehension or perception.

Reconciliation, on the other hand, is a two-way street. Reconciliation is the promise that lies at the heart of forgiveness; it is the full flower of the seed of forgiveness, even when that seed is hidden from sight. The gift of forgiveness will always feel incomplete if it does not bear fruit in reconciliation. This, I am convinced, holds as true in God's forgiveness of us as it does in our forgiveness of one another. Reconciliation means full restoration of a whole relationship, and as such requires conscious mutuality. No reconciliation can take place unless the offender recognizes the offense, desires to be forgiven, and is willing to receive forgiveness. Thus, the role of acknowledgment and confession of sin belongs to the dynamic of forgiveness in relation to reconciliation, not to forgiveness alone.

The Effects of Our Reluctance

It is worth exploring further the effects of our frequent, if peculiar, inability to receive forgiveness, as well as our resistance to offering it.

The willingness to receive forgiveness poses a special challenge. Just as we sometimes take back our forgiveness of another person, we frequently take our sins back from God's release of them. Douglas Steere speaks to this perverse dynamic of human pride and control:

> *There is . . . a condition for receiving God's gift of forgiveness. [We] must be willing to accept it. Absurd as this may seem, there are few who will believe in and accept the forgiveness of God so completely as to . . . leave their sin with [God] forever. They are always re-opening the vault where they have deposited their sin, . . . forever asking to have it back in order to fondle it, to reconstruct, to query, to worry over it. . . . Thus their sin ties them to the past.*[1]

Our reluctance to offer forgiveness also ties us to the past and impedes both the present moment and the future potential of life. My lack of forgiveness holds me captive as much as it keeps another person in subjugation to my conscious and unconscious resentment. The Latin word for mercy is very revealing in this regard. *Eleison* literally means to *unbind*, as our related English word *liaison* means *bond*. When we refuse to forgive, we hold others firmly enmeshed in the bondage of our judgment; when we forgive, we loose others from the attachments of our anger and vengefulness, freeing ourselves in the process.

A most interesting series of meditations on the Syrian Aramaic version of the Lord's Prayer renders this dynamic quite vividly. Here are just a few possible translations of the petition on forgiveness, based on various connotations of the Aramaic words Jesus might have spoken:

> *Loose the cords of mistakes binding us,*
> *as we release the strands we hold of others' guilt.*
> *Lighten our load of secret debts*
> *as we relieve others of their need to repay.*

Forgive our hidden past, the secret shames,
as we consistently forgive what others hide.

The author of these translations speaks eloquently of forgiveness as a "gift we can give one another, an opportunity to let go of the mistakes that tie ourselves and one another in knots."[2] Indeed, it is this feeling of being "knotted up" with someone that makes forgiveness an experience of liberation for both parties.

This may give us a deeper glimpse into those peculiar words Jesus speaks in Matthew 18:18, "Whatever you bind on earth will be bound in heaven, and whatever you loose on earth will be loosed in heaven." If we insist on remaining bound to someone in resentment, heaven will not force us to change our minds. If we remain unwilling to forgive those who wound us, how can God set us free from the knot of a twisted relationship? God wants more than anything to free us. That is why "the Word became flesh and dwelt among us, full of grace and truth" (John 1:14-15, RSV)—to give us a way out of our impenetrable morass of sin. But if we refuse to pass the gift of grace along to those in our debt, we prevent the grace of God's forgiveness from entering our own lives fully. Then what is bound on earth remains bound in heaven, not by God's design but our own.

From this it seems clear that the one condition set for our receiving God's forgiveness is that we also forgive one another. This condition is implied in the wording of the Lord's Prayer: "forgive us our sins as we forgive those who sin against us." It would also appear to be the import of the parable of the unforgiving servant in Matthew 18:23-35. Again, it is not that God, in ornery fashion, is bent on punishing our hard hearts. It is simply that an unforgiving heart of itself blocks the mystery of divine grace. It cannot freely receive what God freely gives. Our openness to God and our openness to one another are thus intrinsically linked.

IT OFTEN HAPPENS BY INCHES
Kathleen Fischer

Some years ago I heard a story about how small actions can bring about large changes. I return to it often for inspiration when I work with families struggling to forgive and reconcile. As the tale opens, two birds, a dove and a coal-mouse, perch on the slim branch of a tree one winter's day. They begin to speak.

"Tell me the weight of a snowflake," a coal-mouse asked a wild dove.

"Nothing more than nothing," was the answer.

"In that case, I must tell you a marvelous story," the coal-mouse said.

"I sat on the branch of a fir, close to its trunk, when it began to snow—not heavily, not in a raging blizzard—no, just like in a dream, without a wound and without any violence. Since I did not have anything better to do, I counted the snowflakes settling on the twigs and needles of my branch. Their number was exactly 3,741,952. When the 3,741,953rd dropped onto the branch, nothing more than nothing, as you say—the branch broke off."

Having said that, the coal-mouse flew away.

The dove, since Noah's time an authority on the matter, thought about the story for awhile and finally said to herself, "Perhaps there is only one person's voice lacking for peace to come to the world."[1]

The same is true of peace in our relationships. Perhaps all that is missing is one word or action. Simple gestures accumulate like snowflakes, each adding its weight to the healing process. Tentative and partial at first, peace gradually grows stronger.

We may think that forgiveness must be 100 percent to make a difference, like an A+ on a perfect paper. In that case, we reason, it is useless to try. There is no way we can reach that goal. But, in fact, moving toward 50 percent or even 10 percent counts. There are degrees of forgiveness. The key is to start somewhere and to keep trying. Decide not only what you can't do but what you can do. Here are some small steps to consider.

Entertain the Possibility

"Forgive him? You've got to be kidding! I couldn't possibly do that."

"Not her! Never. She's got to realize what she did to me."

I hear responses like these when I suggest that forgiveness might provide a way out of personal and family misery. I hesitate at times even to introduce the word. However, forgiveness, always a fundamental Christian ideal, is coming into its own in the field of counseling. Even therapists who dismissed it in the past recognize forgiveness as not only a religious goal but also a powerful path to physical and emotional well-being.

When we experience especially painful wounds, it may be a while before we can bear to hear the word *forgiveness*, but the time comes when we are ready. Speaking of cruel treatment from a relative, a woman says: "I'm not in any hurry to forgive. I have no agenda in that regard. But I do notice a softening of my anger. Something is forgiven inside me. It's more of a grace than something I will to happen. I'm not directing my energy toward him so much anymore."

While it is not our place to tell others they must forgive, we can entertain the possibility at any moment and see where it takes us. The first step may be the realization that we are now strong enough that the person cannot hurt us anymore. Or we may start to feel some small amount of empathy. We can build on these small beginnings.

Give the Offender Credit for Trying

We owe it to others to allow them a fresh start. People can and do change. A daughter remembers her father's relentless criticism as she grew; now she sees him softening as he ages. "He is trying really hard. He's less competitive and angry. What I appreciate is that he keeps coming back to the table to talk again." Or a woman speaks of her friend: "I can't quite trust that she has changed. But I keep telling myself, 'She's trying. Just meet her there.'"

People deserve credit for their past deeds as well. Recall something good about the relationship; acknowledge one positive quality in the person. Perhaps the in-law who hurt you was there for you when you needed help after surgery. When we recognize one another's efforts, goodwill gradually builds.

Pray for Those in Conflict

We don't always think of praying for those locked in a dispute. When we hear that a brother is divorcing or two friends aren't speaking, we may get caught up in taking sides. Instead we can lift them up to God, sending each one love and strength in the Spirit. Such prayers might go something like this:

> May the wisdom of the Spirit be with each of you.
> May your hearts be open to the grace of healing.
> O God, our refuge, protect and guide them.
> God of love, show them the way to love.

Prayer addresses the helplessness we feel when relationships seem to be unraveling. Each time we hear more of the pain and impasse, we can take the matter to prayer once again.

Take Advantage of Opportunities That Arise

"Sometimes something good comes from something bad," an older woman tells me. When illness or misfortune strikes, we have a chance to be there for another who may believe that no one cares. New situations are also possible when a family member or friend gets treatment for diseases like depression and alcoholism. A man comments that his brother is so much easier to relate to now that he is on medication for chronic depression: "He was hypersensitive and held grudges we didn't even know about. He was always angry, and now he's not angry anymore." When individuals choose health, friends and family can find it as well.

Several years ago I worked with a woman who came to our nursing center convinced that she was completely alone in the world and would die that way. However, when I told several nieces and nephews of her predicament, they came through for her. In the months before her death, they visited regularly. They were at her bedside around the clock in her final days.

These nieces and nephews had matured over the years, and they no longer took for granted the interest their aunt had taken in them and the money she had spent on their educations. She, in turn, was able to let go of her resentment over being neglected. Her forgiveness allowed her to die in peace and brought healing to several generations of her family.

Restoration of a relationship is sometimes much more partial than this. In his memoir, *An American Requiem: God, My Father, and the War That Came Between Us*, James Carroll movingly describes such an experience. His father was an air force lieutenant general. James became a priest, his father's pride and joy. Then he protested the Vietnam War. His and his father's strong opposing stances on the war tore apart their family. Years later his father was diagnosed with Alzheimer's disease. At the end, James sat with him for hours, the tension between them now gone, the bad feelings a part of the past. Though his father no longer recognized him, James shaved and bathed him, told him stories, and talked about a novel he was writing. His father listened without being offended. James concludes, "It was the next best thing to being reconciled."[2]

Lower Your Expectations of Others

Close friends and family members hold one another to high standards of behavior. Lowering these expectations leaves room for forgiveness. What does our accumulated wisdom tell us about our close relationships? They will not meet all our needs, even some important ones. Loved ones will make mistakes and sin. Conflict is a normal part of relationships. In every close relationship we experience crisis from time to time.

The people in our lives include the chronic complainers, the relentlessly critical, the boring, the demanding, and the self-absorbed. There are those who cannot listen and those who are too quiet to suit us. We likely fall into several of these categories ourselves. Accepting this fact can relieve much stress and disappointment.

High expectations are the seedbed of harsh judgment. We cannot forgive those who fail to measure up. It helps to turn expectations into preferences, hopes, wishes, or desires: "I would prefer that you be more positive." "I would like it better if you got here on time." "I hope you will get a job soon."

If we can let go, we can enjoy these persons more. Wisdom entails knowing how to adjust to certain realities that will not change. Wisdom is also knowing what to overlook.

Continue Sending Cards, Calls, and E-Mails

A frozen relationship seldom thaws all at once. More often it is a slow melt. For example, a woman sends her sister-in-law an invitation to her daughter's baptism, even though the rest of the family usually excludes her from family events. A daughter announces a small breakthrough in relating to her mother: "I'm so proud of myself. I called my mother last Sunday. I'd been secretly planning to do it for some time, but I didn't tell anyone. I didn't want to feel like I had to do it." She goes on to say that she called when she knew her mom would have company arriving shortly; she did not want it to be a long call that would get them both into old patterns. She had managed to reconnect with her mother, but she had set a boundary. She feels pleased with her progress.

When we send news or photos, call, or write, we convey the message that we want a connection with this person. We keep the door open.

Practice the Art of Listening

Hurts leave us eager to make our own points. Feeling heard and understood, however, generally leads to reconciliation. Listening is an act of caring, and we can offer it to others even when we do not feel any love for them. A daughter, on returning from a visit with her father, said: "It went better this time. I realized that in the past I was too busy judging to be able to really hear him." Even persons we dislike can be the object of this kind of respect, the same respect we hope to receive from them.

These small moments make peace possible in difficult relationships. It would be wonderful if forgiveness and reconciliation occurred instantaneously and lasted forever. The time and effort they take discourage us. But throughout the Gospels small things matter; they become the seeds of larger moments of grace. Our efforts, though seemingly insignificant, open us to the movement of the Spirit. The important thing is to begin, trusting the rest to God's promise of transformation.

RELEASE TO NEW HEALING CHOICES
Flora Slosson Wuellner

In this wounded and wounding world we will always be in some less-than-perfect relationships. Among the tough choices we make within healthy forgiveness is choosing to honor ourselves enough to expect courtesy and faith-keeping from those with whom we live and work. If these expectations are violated, it is part of forgiveness to make clear, gently but firmly, what we will and will not tolerate. This stance is especially essential if we are returning to a relationship in which former hurts are healing.

Setting Valid Limits

In her book *The Verbally Abusive Relationship*, therapist Pat Evans points out that verbal abuse is not the same as ordinary conflict. Conflict is a disagreement regarding interests or the result of poor communication skills, which often can be resolved by those who together seek reasonable solutions. But abuse (of any kind) is a violation and a deliberate demeaning of another, which cannot be healed by reasonable discussion or even by the usual forms of counseling. This root difference explains why marriage, family, or job counseling so often fails. Abusiveness is an addiction to power exerted over another, and mere communication skills do not heal it. Setting limits is absolutely necessary in such cases.

Evans points out that a simple, firm "stop it" is effective when the demeaning remarks begin. This approach does not mean that the people involved cannot discuss problems; it means that such discussion must be held with mutual respect.

Setting our valid limits definitely includes our firm, unapologetic claiming of the space and time we need for self-care and self-renewal. We have the need as well as the right to be in silence at times, to be alone at times, to think things over in our own way at our own pace, to enter into our "sabbaths" of relaxation and enjoyment. Self-care is not at all the same as selfishness. A selfish person who needs to grab and put "me first" on all occasions is usually a person who does not understand healthy self-care and the dignity of one's true needs.

If we want forgiveness for our own past trespasses upon others, we need to ask God to help us understand why we have violated the freedom, dignity, and spaces of others. Were our own boundaries violated as a child? Do we demean others because we feel vulnerable and threatened if we don't? What are our bodily and emotional signals when we feel the urge to dominate and invade others? If we have a deep, chronic problem in our relationships, we probably will need professional therapeutic help to answer these questions. We will also need deep, healing prayer and the prayer of others, for this is a deep wound in ourselves that inflicts dangerous wounds on others.

Speaking the Truth in Love

I have read that for a former victim of an abusive situation to tell even one small lie to keep the peace is as dangerous as an alcoholic's taking one small drink.

We cannot afford any inner or outer deceptions about what is really happening, how we really feel, what we will and will not accept. Abuses of any kind depend on cover-ups. Any form of communal or individual forgiveness that consents to cover-ups is not forgiveness at all; it is corruption!

The truth must be named. As Jesus said, "Nothing is covered up that will not be uncovered, and nothing secret that will not become known" (Luke 12:2).

Telling the truth does not mean vituperative yells. Emotional explosions usually make matters less clear, not more. Nor does telling the truth mean that we ignore the needs and feelings of others, even of our former abusers. We listen, trying to hear their heart, but we do not permit verbal or emotional violation. We keep right on speaking clearly about what we see happening and how we choose to act.

Suppose, for example, we choose to attend a reunion of our dysfunctional family, in which hurts are whispered about behind closed doors, and whatever is spoken aloud is usually a way of saying "you fool." How do we speak the truth in love in such an atmosphere?

First, we can ask the risen Christ to go ahead of us and prepare that potentially painful place for us and to stand with us as we enter that hurting and hurtful group. We might even ask him to stand between us and another person who may be draining us of energy or projecting hurtfulness on us.

When a family member whispers to us the latest mean thing someone else has said or done, we can reflect back to that person just what we are hearing. "This is what I am hearing you say, Aunt. How do you feel about it? What do you intend to do about it?" This neither makes excuses for the one responsible for the injury nor affirms the victimhood of the person confiding in us.

If another family member begins to make demeaning jokes, we can say, "I wonder what you are really feeling as you tell this hurtful joke. This is the way it makes me feel. . . ."

If another member of the family starts complaining and criticizing who we are or what we are doing, we can respond: "I'm sorry for both of us that you don't approve, but this is the way I see it, and this is my choice. If we can't talk it over with respect for each other, we'd better talk about something else."

Learning to respond with goodwill and clear firmness within a hurtful relationship can be as scary to a former victim as walking up to a hungry lion! To tell the truth in situations where we used to apologize, explain, prevaricate, blow up, flee in tears? Surely there will be disaster! There will only be fragmented pieces of us left!

Usually, in fact, we will be amazed at the power of good-humored truth telling. It will often be for us as it was for the prophet Daniel so many centuries ago, standing in the den of lions: "My God sent his angel and shut the lions' mouths so that they would not hurt me" (Daniel 6:22). Others are so often totally taken by surprise at hearing the truth spoken calmly and clearly that they will back off speechless or even be shocked into an honest, reflective response. If abusive reactions do continue, we can exercise our firm limit-setting by merely smiling and walking away, saying, "I don't choose to stay with this."

When it comes to forgiveness given and received between wounding communities, churches, nations, political parties, ethnic groups, systems and organizations of all kinds, the truth must be spoken. It is definitely not enough to name the crimes of the past. They must be remembered and the naming must be continued at intervals. "Eternal vigilance is the price of liberty" is an old saying of profound wisdom. All communal powers without exception (including all religious communal bodies) are tempted constantly to violate, to trespass. The tragic irony is that the more sincere and idealistic the violators, the more they are tempted to trespass, to use force over others, to seek dominance over the inner spirit and not just the outer action, all for the "higher good" of those they are violating.

Trying to forgive a hurtful community or nation is useless unless the truth of its history is remembered, its truth told, and unless there are definite signs of its repentance, its turning around.

Should All Things Be Forgiven?

Are some acts unforgivable? How can one even think of forgiving ethnic holocausts? Isn't it obscene even to think of forgiving abuse of helpless children? How can anyone forgive the deliberate ruin of another person's life? These agonizing questions cannot be treated either sentimentally or superficially in the name of forgiveness.

Acts of cruelty and evil cannot be condoned or forgiven. The history of an act cannot be changed. It has done its work. Nor can the evil, dehumanizing ideologies that gave rise to those acts be forgiven. Rigid and loveless theologies, commercial greed, fanatical political and ethnic mind-sets that have led to inquisitions, witch-hunts, slave trading, and holocausts are unforgivable. God and the human wills set free by God eventually will dissolve these ideologies. Communal powers, nations, churches, industrial and political organizations that allow themselves to be corrupted by these dehumanizing ideologies and do not repent—turn around—also will be dissolved.

In the vision of time's end (Matt. 25:31-46), Jesus speaks of the nations gathered before God for discernment and judgment (verse 32), a judgment of communal powers, not individuals. Communal powers that have neglected and abused the vulnerable, the helpless, the hungry, and have not reformed will not survive. How many civilizations of the world already have been lost and forgotten?

God does not dissolve the individual. We stay in our self-made hell as long as we choose, as long as we ignore God's hand stretched out to help us. One of C. S. Lewis's books *The Great Divorce* describes in fictional form how the souls in hell may take a bus to heaven whenever they choose. The spirits of the blessed meet them and plead with them to stay in heaven, but most of them choose to return to their self-made hell because they are more comfortable in their glumness, self-pity, resentments, and because they are frightened at the bigness and solid realness of heaven and the painful growth required to become real and full of light.

As far as God is concerned, God still speaks to each of us as "my child." Jesus does speak of a sin that cannot be forgiven:

> Truly I tell you, people will be forgiven for their sins and whatever blasphemies they utter; but whoever blasphemes against the Holy Spirit can never have forgiveness, but is guilty of an eternal sin. (Mark 3:28-29)

If we understand the Holy Spirit, the Paraclete, as "the one who stands beside us, and calls us forth," this saying becomes more clear. If we refuse to turn to that one who stands by us, refuse that love and outstretched hand, if we refuse to come forth from our inner prisons—then there is no way we can be helped. We have refused the offered forgiveness, and thus it cannot heal our lives.

When we are the victims of radical evil, we are not asked to forgive the evil act. We are asked to remember that the perpetrator, even though trapped for now in the evil, is nonetheless a child of God. Even when we cannot yet forgive and release that other child of God, and perhaps cannot do so for a long time, we can deliver that person into God's hands, saying, "Loving God, at this time my hurt is so deep and my heart is so devastated with pain that I cannot even begin to forgive this person. It is enough for now to know that my wounder is in your hands, even as I am, and with you there is perfect understanding and recompense for all my pain. When the time is right, help me to begin my journey of healing and release." Such a prayer is already well within the great unfolding of forgiveness.

Is Restitution Possible?

Even if an abuser or violator has shown remorse; proved repentance by changing his or her direction; assumed financial responsibility for what has happened; told the truth to all involved; and given time, thought, and energy to repairing the damages, can the damage ever be undone?

In a sense we cannot ever make up for what we have done. Something real has been lost. Harm has happened. For example, if a person has experienced years of childhood neglect and rejection, a normal, happy childhood for that person is lost forever. The parents, even if fully aware and repentant, cannot restore that lost childhood even if a later relationship has become healed and close. Betrayal, infidelity to a spouse or friend, cannot be undone.

I neglected a dear friend once in the daily busyness of my life. She sent me a message saying she would like to see me. I thoroughly intended to go, but all sorts of other things came up I needed to attend to. I kept putting it off. Then she died, without having seen me. I realized then what I had left undone. My excuses were good ones, and knowing her, I knew she forgave me. Still, nothing could ever change the fact that I was not there by her bedside when she needed me. My choice became part of the universe, a fact that stood. "Forgive us our debts. . . ." This was a debt I could not ever repay.

Forgiveness cannot change the past. But lest we feel that God has no answer other than to love us yet leave us with a sense of eternal loss, consider this bold vision: "So if anyone is in Christ, there is a new creation: everything old has passed away; see, everything has become new!" (2 Corinthians 5:17).

We are told that though our choices stand as unchangeable facts in the old universe, God offers us a new universe. We are still responsible for trying to make what restitution we can, for trying to heal wounds we have inflicted, but the crushing burden of guilt is lifted from us. The prison door is open, and that place we used to live is no longer our home. We are no longer the persons we were then. Who knows but that God will give us the joy of some new morning in a new vineyard to work within God's love!

The best reparation we can offer is to become compassionate toward those who mistreat us the way we mistreated others, releasing them from resentment. For example, the only true reparation I could make to my old friend whom I had neglected was to become more understanding of anybody who neglected me. Instead of taking offense at a friend who had forgotten or who was too busy to call or write me, I would try to remember how often I too had become distracted and overwhelmed by daily chores and neglected others. Then I would try to release that friend from the prison of my offendedness. I believe my old friend's beautiful spirit touched mine with this guidance. I remember the relief I felt when I realized I could do something real and valuable "in remembrance" of her.

This does *not* mean, however, that we should submit to abuse and victimization as reparation. Some years ago I knew of a son who had wounded his mother deeply with neglect and verbal abuse. He finally realized what was happening, repented, got professional help, and tried to become a loving, loyal son to her. In his remorse he went too far, turning himself into a slave to her every whim. Their relationship quickly became a toxic one, as she increasingly became the dictator and he the remorseful victim, forever trying to make up his earlier neglect of her. This is not righteous reparation; this is sickness. He did not understand or claim the dignity of a forgiven child of God but let his needs and valid boundaries be violated.

Sooner or later within our adventure of forgiveness, we will need to release our expectation that past history can be changed or compensated. It is an enormous step when we finally can say and believe: "That is past. Yes, something was lost, and harm was done. I grieve for it. But now, reborn within God's heart, I am in my true home. I am in a different spiritual and emotional universe. I see with different eyes and feast on new possibilities. I am a new person now,

for God has called me 'out of darkness into his marvelous light'"
(1 Peter 2:9).

This awareness, this good news, is the deep fulfillment of our hunger and thirst for righteousness.

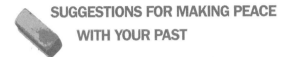

SUGGESTIONS FOR MAKING PEACE
WITH YOUR PAST

1

Forgive yourself. Sometimes we're harder on ourselves than we are on other people. Take a few minutes at the end of each week to let go of words or deeds you wish you had handled differently.

2

Write that letter to someone you've been meaning to forgive. Even if you don't mail it, chances are you'll feel better after putting your thoughts on paper.

3

Allow your friends and family members to make mistakes. As painful as it is to be hurt by someone close to you, try to remember that nobody's perfect.

4

Think about how you'd like to be forgiven yourself. Can you offer the same gesture to someone else?

5

Remember that forgiving does not mean pretending that the offensive act never happened. However, letting go of the resentment will make it easier for you to forgive.

6

Ask yourself if you need to seek forgiveness from anyone you've harmed. Make a plan for the best way to approach the person.

7

For those moments you wish you could "do over," think about how you would handle similar situations in the future.

8

Accept the fact that you can't control the outcome when you reach out to ask for forgiveness. All you can do is make the first move.

9

Talk to a church official or professional counselor if you're burdened by an act so offensive you don't think you can ever forgive the perpetrator.

10

Don't panic if forgiveness does not come easily to you. With enough practice, you'll become comfortable with letting go of past hurts.

NOTES

INTRODUCTION, Amy Lyles Wilson

Epigraph. Lewis B. Smedes, *Forgive and Forget: Healing the Hurts We Don't Deserve* (San Francisco: HarperSanFrancisco, 1996), 39.

WHAT FORGIVENESS IS AND IS NOT, Kenneth Gibble

1. Barbara Brown Taylor, *Gospel Medicine* (Cambridge, MA: Cowley Publications, 1995), xx.

HOW DO I PROTECT MYSELF?, Kathleen Fischer

1. The story of the snake is told by Fred Luskin, *Forgive for Good: A Proven Prescription for Health and Happiness* (New York: HarperCollins Publishers, 2003), 192.

2. C. S. Lewis, *The Four Loves* (London: Fontana Books, 1963), 111.

OUR RESISTANCE TO FORGIVENESS, Marjorie J. Thompson

1. Douglas V. Steere, *Dimensions of Prayer* (New York: Women's Division of the Board of Global Ministries, United Methodist Church, 1962), 56–57.

2. Neil Douglas-Klotz, *Prayers of the Cosmos* (San Francisco: Harper and Row, 1990), 30–31.

IT OFTEN HAPPENS BY INCHES, Kathleen Fischer

1. The tale of the dove and the coal-mouse is from Joseph Jaworski, *Synchronicity: The Inner Path of Leadership*, ed. Betty Sue Flowers (San Francisco: Berrett-Koehler Publishers, 1998), 197.

2. James Carroll, *An American Requiem: God, My Father, and the War That Came Between Us* (Boston: Houghton Mifflin Company, 1996), 262.

Contributors

Jean M. Blomquist is a freelance writer and editor who lives with her husband near San Francisco.

Elizabeth J. Canham, an Episcopal priest, is also an author, retreat leader, spiritual director, and former seminary professor.

Kathleen Fischer works as a psychotherapist and spiritual director in Seattle. She is the author of several books, including *Forgiving Your Family: A Journey to Healing* and *Winter Grace: Spirituality and Aging*.

Kenneth Gibble, a retired pastor, now writes poetry and stories instead of sermons.

Henri J. M. Nouwen, 1932–1996, was an internationally respected author, priest, and professor.

Roberta Porter is a retired teacher who lives on the Oregon coast with her husband. She is the mother of three and the grandmother of nine.

Mary Lou Redding is editorial director of *The Upper Room* daily devotional guide and author of *Breaking and Mending: Divorce and God's Grace*, among other books.

Douglas V. Steere, 1901–1995, was a leading Quaker theologian and authority on the spiritual life. He authored numerous books, including *Dimensions of Prayer* and *Together in Solitude*.

Marjorie J. Thompson is director of the Pathways Center for Christian Spirituality at Upper Room Ministries in Nashville, Tennessee, and the author of *Soul Feast* and *Family the Forming Center*.

Amy Lyles Wilson is a writer, editor, and workshop leader in Nashville, Tennessee. She is a graduate of Millsaps College, the University of Mississippi, and Vanderbilt University Divinity School. An affiliate of Amherst Writers and Artists, her byline has appeared in publications including *The Spire* and *Weavings: A Journal of the Christian Spiritual Life*.

Wendy M. Wright is professor of Theology and holds the John F. Kenefick Chair in the Humanities at Creighton University in Omaha, Nebraska. She writes about the history of Christian spirituality, family spirituality, and women's spirituality.

Flora Slosson Wuellner, an ordained minister of the United Church of Christ, is well known for her writings and retreat leadership that focus on the inner healing that God freely offers through Christ. Author of *Forgiveness, the Passionate Journey* and *Prayer, Stress, and Our Inner Wounds*.